Narcissism

Strategically Disengage From A Codependent Partnership
And Confidently Address The Behaviors Of A
Narcissistic Individual

*(Traversing Relationships With Narcissistic Traits And
Embracing A Journey Of Recovery And Self- Care)*

Clifford Turnbull

TABLE OF CONTENT

What Constitutes Codependency And What Falls Outside Its Parameters? 1

What is Codependency? 1

Narcissistic Abuse 22

Healthy And Unhealthy Narcissism 45

Addressing Traumatic Brain Injuries And Facilitating Recovery 82

What Is The Manifestation Of Narcissistic Traits? 102

The Fundamental Element For Attaining Mastery 116

Diagnosis Of Narcissism 144

What Constitutes Codependency And What Falls Outside Its Parameters?

What is Codependency?

The term 'codependency' may appear to denote a positive concept, signifying a mutually advantageous relationship. Should you have harbored initial positive impressions upon encountering the term, rest assured that you are not the sole individual to have done so. Certainly, codependency does imply a certain level of reciprocity, but the notion of it being advantageous is entirely inaccurate.

A codependent relationship does not offer any advantages, nor does it provide any benefits for individuals caught in codependency. Certainly, an individual who exhibits codependency is someone whose internal relationship is characterized by profound self-doubt, leading to a loss of self-trust. Upon the termination of a codependent relationship, it is probable that one of the individuals involved will exhibit tendencies towards self-harm, self-condemnation, self-stigmatization, and an incapacity to effectively manage even the most minor instances of criticism. This commonly serves as a precursor to engaging in self-sabotaging or potentially self-destructive behaviors, including instances of suicidal ideation.

Codependency, in its fundamental manifestation, denotes an excessive proclivity towards psychological or emotional dependence on another individual necessitating assistance due to addiction or compromised well-being. A codependent individual is someone who acquiesces to the actions of another person to such an extent that they assume complete accountability for regulating the behavior of the other person. The codependent individual serves as an enabler for the dependent individual within the context of their relationship. To articulate further, the partner who is codependent exhibits behaviors that inadvertently reinforce and enable their counterpart in indulging in their lack of accountability, immaturity, addiction, and illness.

Codependency extends beyond mere tendencies of emotional attachment. A codependent individual generally tends to center their existence on their partner, with their own world revolving around the world of the partner. They undertake extraordinary measures to satisfy their significant other. A codependent relationship is characterized by the perception of one partner that their sense of purpose hinges upon the provision of support to the other individual, while the other individual holds the belief that they must be indispensable. The codependent partner often demonstrates selfless behavior for the benefit of their partner who, coincidentally, demands nothing less. The cycle of codependency refers to the mutual dependency that arises when one partner exhibits excessive dependency while the other seeks validation through being relied upon.

Codependency extends beyond the confines of exclusive romantic relationships. It is a possibility that such occurrences can manifest among acquaintances, relatives, and even coworkers within professional settings. In numerous instances, the relationship has the potential to deteriorate into a physically and emotionally abusive dynamic. Frequently, individuals external to the relationship often possess the ability to readily discern any discord, while the codependent partner typically remains unaware of such indications.

Codependency is not...

Codependency is not caregiving.

Many individuals may experience difficulty distinguishing between the two concepts, as the term has become excessively utilized in our vocabulary. Consequently, nearly all instances of benevolence and supportive behavior are invariably perceived as codependent, despite the existence of a substantial disparity between these two notions. When an individual displays selflessness by attending to the needs of ailing family members, such as parents or offspring.

A significant distinction exists as they are devoting their own selves to that individual out of love and a desire to witness their improvement.

These are specific situations.

This is not a recurrent pattern of relationships and dysfunction actively pursued by them, even if they are not consciously aware of their consistent seeking of such dynamics. One may regard it as akin to a chronic condition versus an acute condition.

In the event that the immediate circumstances transition into sustained attentiveness. The caregiver's dependence is not the determining factor. They are undertaking this act based on their deep affection towards a child, a parent, or any individual involved.

It is crucial to avoid mistaking acts of kindness and affection as signs of codependency.

They are distinct entities.

Certain individuals find themselves in circumstances where they are compelled to make selfless contributions, as highlighted in the aforementioned instances. These individuals do not actively pursue such situations, but rather embrace them wholeheartedly, employing love, empathy, benevolence, and an authentic dedication towards restoring the individuals in question to their original state.

From a different perspective, one could argue that individuals exhibiting codependency tend to gravitate towards it due to familiarity and a lack of alternatives.

It is an inherent urge to engage in a relationship characterized by one's commitment to wholeheartedly cater to, protect, or exert dominance over the other individual.

It does not originate from a foundation of compassion.

The behavior arises from a state of necessity, as the codependent individual seeks to fulfill their own longing for acceptance and validation through their association with this person.

Conversely, the individual providing care is motivated by sincere affection, concern, and benevolence. They are engaged in this behavior out of a strong sense of duty to assist a cherished individual, rather than it being an act of compulsion.

It is of utmost importance to discern the two and comprehend the distinction. It denotes a well-established and constructive reaction to a family member or friend requiring assistance, devoid of any underlying motivations to fulfill personal desires or compulsions.

It is intended to provide assistance and caregiving to those individuals whom they hold dear.

The interdependency stems from a sense of shame. They will refute their own needs and feelings. They exhibit a meticulous approach when it comes to assisting the individual with whom they are engaged. Their continued presence is attributed to their lack of self-confidence, as well as an incessant desire to seek approval from others and experience feelings of remorse if they are unable to meet exceedingly high standards. This is codependency.

The boundaries are significantly disproportionate.

Meanwhile, the person in good health is seeking to provide care for the individual. They are engaging in this action fueled by a deep sense of affection. They are engaging in these actions driven by an authentic sense of care, concern, and benevolence.

Codependency represents an artificial approximation of the authentic nature of genuine love. It manifests as an intense and overwhelming desire to constantly seek the approval, validation, and admiration of others.

Merely possessing the inclination to support others and be present for one's loved ones does not give rise to codependency.

In conclusion, codependency does not entail merely providing care and unconditional support to the people we deeply care about, but rather, involves an earnest desire to witness their happiness and assist them during challenging phases of their lives. Furthermore, such instances do not pertain to instances where one experiences fleeting pain due to a betrayal, nor do they align with our desire to witness someone's growth and progress as they engage in detrimental behaviors.

These are normal reactions.

This is an inherent aspect of the human experience.

Codependence, Dependence, and Interdependence

It is not infrequent for individuals to mistakenly conflate interdependent relationships with codependent ones. This perplexity arises from the notion that the individuals within a perfect relationship ought to rely on one another. Though the validity of that notion is partially true, excessive reliance on another individual can prove to be adverse in various circumstances. Children and pets are inherently reliant on their parents and owners, leaving them with no alternative but to depend entirely on them. However, for adults, depending entirely on a spouse, friend, or superior may not be a prudent course of action.

It may be deemed imperative to furnish a concise elucidation of the affiliated terminologies (with regard to relationships) in order to engender enhanced comprehensibility.

• Reliance: This pertains to a heightened level of dependence and placing significant trust in another individual. It may give rise to excessive emotional dependency and vulnerability to individuals with controlling tendencies. A person who relies heavily on another individual displays an unusually high level of tolerance due to an anticipated advantage.

• Autonomy: An autonomous individual possesses the ability to direct oneself. He or she is not beholden to external governance or swayed by external influences. A partnership characterized by complete autonomy for each individual may encounter formidable difficulties that cannot be overcome. Partners who exhibit interdependence regardless of their individual capacity for self-sufficiency have a higher likelihood of prospering in collaboration.

- Mutual Dependence: This refers to a state of interdependency. It represents a harmonious balance achieved through skillful integration of interdependence and autonomy. Put differently, the concept of interdependence within relationships entails a constructive reliance on one another.

- Codependency: This term denotes the psychological or emotional dependence on another individual, exceeding healthy boundaries of interdependence. A codependent individual obtains their sense of self through engaging in behaviors that seek approval.

Discerning the Contrast: Codependency versus Interdependency

As mature individuals, we rely on others to engage in sexual intimacy, cultivate friendships, foster love, facilitate communication, allow for physical contact, and express appreciation. We relinquish our authentic sense of self when we consent to enduring mistreatment at the hands of others in order to satisfy these desires. Rather than satisfying their social, emotional, and sexual needs, their insecurities hinder their ability to derive pleasure from these experiences. In a relationship characterized by codependency, it is common for one or both partners to experience perpetual apprehension regarding the potential loss of the other individual, as they believe they lack the ability to operate independently. They experience a sense of confinement and harboring frustration; however, they are under the impression that they are unable to take any action to address this predicament. Fear also serves as a deterrent to emotional intimacy, even in instances where individuals engage in physical intimacy. Typically, they tend to find it arduous to unwind and lower their defenses, thus making themselves susceptible to one another.

Conversely, a mutually dependent association is indicative of a robust and positive dynamic. The contradiction inherent in interdependent relationships arises from their occurrence between individuals who possess autonomy. The individuals possess the liberty to express their authentic selves while acknowledging the interdependence necessary for the success of their relationship. Partners in a resilient and mutually supportive relationship hold a deep regard for each other's individuality and personal identity. There exists no obligation for the other individual involved in the relationship to relinquish or compromise their own set of values.

A robust interdependence is established when individuals or pairs within a relationship achieve equilibrium between extreme reliance and overwhelming autonomy. They are cognizant of the fact that their inherent human requirement for interconnectedness can solely be fulfilled within a conducive environment of interdependence. They adopt an approach to their relationships that resembles a cooperative alliance or joint venture. Similar to a partnership, the successful functioning of a couple in a wholesome relationship necessitates an understanding of the significance of mutual respect in preserving their bond and allowing it to thrive.

The profound affection between individuals can elicit a longing for intimacy and give the impression that they are inseparable; however, it is crucial to distinguish this from the notion of codependency. Responsibility and power are among the primary distinctions observed when contrasting a codependent relationship with an interdependent one.

Codependent individuals bear the burden of assuming responsibility for their respective partners. They harbor a sense of accountability towards their partner's emotional states, sentiments, and conduct. There tend to be power dynamics at play in their relationship, with each partner vying for control or attempting to influence the behavior of the other individual.

Conversely, interdependent couples solely take accountability for their actions, emotional states, and sentiments. Given their equal distribution of power, there is minimal scope for exerting control or engaging in emotional manipulation. There is no need for them to manipulate or persuade the other individual in order to perceive their own value. Their well-being is not contingent upon dictating the behavior of others to align with their preferences. They both exhibit reciprocal admiration and offer unwavering assistance in pursuit of their respective and shared objectives. Due to their possession of favorable self-perception, they exhibit a willingness to engage in candid and transparent communication. This facilitates a more open and receptive environment for their mutual communication, promoting a sense of empathy and understanding instead of defensiveness or guilt. Furthermore, fulfilling their social, emotional, and sexual needs proves to be a straightforward accomplishment for them, as the absence of any apprehension towards intimacy allows for a seamless and uninhibited connection among individuals.

Discerning Codependency and Dependency: Is there a Distinction?

The codependent reinforces the dependent by providing care and support, thereby attempting to resolve their issues. In certain cases, the dependent may experience incapacitation as a result of poor health. In alternate scenarios, the state of helplessness is cultivated gradually through an extended duration of being enabled.

In this context, the term 'codependency' denotes a situation where one individual relies on the other for their own emotional healing, while the other individual derives a sense of self-worth from resolving the issues of the former. The codependent partner's self-esteem and self-worth are intricately tied to their ability to assist others, make personal sacrifices, and appease others under the guise of being proactive. Over a period of time, individuals of this kind gradually relinquish their authentic sense of identity due to their inability to fully embrace their genuine emotions and exercise their independent judgment. A codependent individual may harbor significant displeasure towards something; however, due to their inability to take ownership of their emotions, they would demonstrate tolerance if their dependent partner exhibits a liking for it. As an illustration, an individual with codependent tendencies might express something along the lines of, "Though I am not particularly inclined towards individuals of a melancholic nature, given that my partner possesses such qualities, I suppose I can devise strategies to adapt and manage." It is possible that I may alter them."

Narcissistic Abuse

Narcissistic abuse refers to a form of psychological mistreatment that is commonly inflicted by a partner exhibiting narcissistic traits and perpetually evading accountability for the origins of intense confrontations. A standard manifestation of narcissistic abuse encompassing recurrent episodes of emotional eruptions, rage, humiliation, derogation, judgment, falsehoods, and intimidation. The victim typically experiences a state of confusion and self-doubt as a result of repeated mistreatment combined with efforts to manipulate and exert control over them.

Certain methods frequently employed in this form of mistreatment include inducing fear in the victim through sudden outbursts and intimidating gazes, instilling uncertainty through falsehoods and deceit, implementing silent treatment as a means of punishment, and manipulating the victim into assuming full responsibility by employing veiled threats of abandonment or by assuming the role of the victim themselves. The indications of being involved in such a relationship are commonly observed in the behavior of one's spouse, the pattern of such mistreatment, and the psychological state of the victim.

Strategies for Healing from the Effects of Narcissistic Abuse

Throughout the years, I have frequently been inquired about the feasibility of achieving complete healing from the effects of narcissistic abuse. At the time those questions were posed, I was uncertain about how to articulate my response. However, upon reflecting upon it now, I have come to the realization that complete recovery from the aforementioned abuse is indeed feasible. Despite the potentially prolonged duration, you will eventually achieve full recovery. Being subjected to narcissistic abuse can give rise to enduring consequences that are profoundly challenging to cope with. Certain outcomes are of trivial nature, whereas others possess the potential to be fatal owing to their magnitude. Several of these adverse reactions encompass temporary memory impairment, fluctuations in mood and temperament, heightened restlessness and agitativeness, intense apprehension and despondency, post-traumatic stress disorder (PTSD), diminished self-esteem, and an unwillingness to grant oneself forgiveness.

In the event that you have experienced or are currently experiencing the detrimental effects of narcissistic abuse, the following measures can be implemented to facilitate your healing process.

Indicate The Abuse:
Detection of abuse could potentially present challenges. Nevertheless, acknowledging the events and affirming your encounters empowers you to maintain a state of objectivity. Please be cognizant of the fact that individuals who engage in abusive behavior are capable of transitioning from displaying extreme cruelty to exhibiting exceptionally affectionate behavior. In public, they often exude an aura of benevolence or compassion. Nevertheless, behaviors such as excessive blame-shifting, public

humiliation, derogatory language, controlling tendencies, and intense possessiveness are all considered to be indicative of abusive conduct.

.

Cut Off Contact:
Seldom, if at all, do abusive relationships exhibit spontaneous improvement. The most optimal course of action for restoring your overall welfare generally involves terminating your relationship with an individual exhibiting narcissistic traits. Due to their inherent disposition, it is probable that they will respond in an erroneous manner. They may attempt to compel your return, offer hollow assurances of your reform, endeavor to undermine your standing within the community, or issue fabricated menaces to jeopardize your prospects.

Define Clear Boundaries:

Adopting a strategy that involves completely refraining from any interaction with the perpetrator of the abuse is often the most advisable approach for facilitating one's recovery. This approach necessitates a significant degree of self-restraint, yet concurrently diminishes the opportunities for establishing a genuine connection and inadvertently falling prey to deceit within the relationship. If it is necessary for ongoing communication to occur (as may be the case in co-parenting situations), it is advisable to establish well-defined and explicit parameters for such correspondence. You are more likely to shield yourself from additional turmoil if you can maintain those limits to a greater extent.

4. Reclaiming your identity:

Narcissistic individuals commonly possess preconceived notions regarding the manner in which others should conduct themselves. They engage in harsh ridicule or censure towards individuals who fail to meet these expectations. They may endeavor to regulate your schedule by disallowing your social interactions or participation in solitary pursuits. One may experience a sense of unfamiliarity with oneself. In the event that this manipulation has resulted in modifications to your physical appearance and personal aesthetics or the loss of cherished belongings, what course of action should you pursue? I would strongly recommend that you proceed with reclaiming your identity. Engage in the activities you once enjoyed prior to experiencing abuse, and dress in the clothing you no longer donned solely due to their requests.

5. Establish goals for oneself:

It is imperative to establish personal objectives. These objectives will provide you with guidance in life and help you maintain a distinct sense of focus. It is of utmost importance to possess a clear sense of purpose, as individuals who exit abusive relationships often experience a profound sense of aimlessness. In order to derive satisfaction and enhance one's self-assurance, it is imperative to ensure consistent commitment to one's goals on a daily basis. The higher your level of self-confidence, the easier it becomes to navigate complex dilemmas and situations.

"A small message that I would appreciate you leaving behind:

Each process of healing will possess its own distinctive qualities, akin to the intricate characteristics of the abuse experienced.

Nevertheless, a definite indication that springs to mind is the diminished impact caused by an unforeseen encounter, a social event, or another individual's enthusiastic endorsement of the perpetrator, no longer evoking a strong or adverse reaction within you. Conversely, you will gradually perceive that your encounters have endowed you with invaluable insights and wisdom, resulting in a notable reduction in your level of animosity, rage, apprehension, and/or inclination for retribution. You are now encouraged to actively pursue meaningful emotional connections elsewhere in a liberated manner.

An additional indication of your recovery is that you begin to experience a sense of emotional buoyancy or a feeling of weightlessness. Occasionally, one is inclined to unconsciously display a smile.

Persistent physical ailments, such as joint pain, abdominal discomfort, and migraines, may occasionally exhibit diminished severity over time.
One can enhance their ability to concentrate and remain fully engaged. You possess a heightened sense of inner harmony and display decreased inclination to evade or deviate from adversities.

Combine Pen and Paper

It can be effortlessly seduced by the ebbs, flows, and exhilaration of a matter without apprehending the true essence of the message conveyed and the essential teachings that necessitate assimilation. However, I guarantee my utmost endeavor to avert such a predicament.

I have instructed the adoption of the practice of introspection as the initial stage in embarking on your path to recovery. The forthcoming pages contain essential lessons that must be acquired and effectively implemented.

It is imperative to possess a written declaration encompassing your well-considered and contemplative reflections, as well as your aspirations and goals. Please take into consideration that it is not possible for you to regain your previous life before the influence of a narcissist. Alternatively, you can have a future that will be significantly more advantageous than your current circumstances.

As the adage states, it is unrealistic to anticipate that past events or experiences would remain unaltered upon revisiting them. It is imperative that you proceed ahead, initially by permitting it within your thoughts, and subsequent to that, by physically executing your intentions.

Imagine this scenario: you have fortuitously stumbled upon a remarkable invention - a time machine of unparalleled capabilities, granting you the extraordinary ability to journey back to your personal history, with the purpose of averting a potentially disastrous occurrence. Upon reflection, you have ascertained that, were it not for this dreadful encounter, your life would have been utterly magnificent. Very well, proceed to embark and have your past rectified.

Presented here is an incident from your previous existence wherein an unfamiliar individual is on the verge of attempting to rob you. You possess the ability to accomplish this and effectively preempted its occurrence. When one engages in historical manipulation, there are resulting ramifications. Due to the modification of that singular occurrence, you refrained from visiting the hospital.

This implies that you failed to establish social connections with Jane. Consequently, you failed to seize the chance to meet and wed Mike, who happens to be an acquaintance of Jane. We inadvertently neglected to mention one final matter, that being the existence of your deeply cherished son that you and Mike father together, which would regrettably cease to be.

Do you continue to hold the belief that it is a worthwhile notion to revisit and eliminate your previous encounters? Considering a more advantageous future, what is your opinion?

There exists a straightforward equation for this particular procedure. Initially, it is imperative to foster the belief that one possesses the ability to supplant any preexisting notions concerning oneself, irrespective of their deeply ingrained nature.

Additionally, it is advisable to formulate a fresh set of values and aspirations as well as envision a revised trajectory for the future. Furthermore, it is imperative to exercise control over any additional thoughts that contradict your newfound conviction.

In conclusion, select the speed that is most suitable for your needs. Either a gradual progression followed by a more rapid escalation or an accelerated approach. This framework offers the potential for success, as it accommodates the pursuit of any aspiration or ambition. Perform the task at hand while diligently observing the transformative effects that ensue upon engaging in such actions.

Discover a serene location in which you may find solitude to contemplate undisturbed. Permit your thoughts to gracefully transcend towards all that you yearn for, whilst you attentively witness yourself within these scenarios. Experience the comforting sensation of his hands enveloping yours as you embark on a leisurely walk; savor the aroma of freshly baked chicken wafting through the air as you join each other for a shared meal. I kindly request that you refrain from relying solely on your memory, as in today's era characterized by an abundance of information and various distractions, it is probable that relying on memory alone may lead to failure.

Please record each scene according to your desired specifications.

Disregard the voice that asserts it as a work of fiction. We have now gained the understanding that we are capable of manifesting the desired life from its initial conceptualization to its ultimate realization.

The practice of documenting one's dreams and aspirations is a vital habit observed by individuals who have achieved exceptional success. This opportunity serves as a means of providing a fresh start to one's life, free from limitations or limited aspirations.

I have likewise transcribed my personal aspirations. Indeed, it is with utmost confidence that I state how, during those initial hours of the morning, when tranquility envelops my thoughts and surroundings, I obtain the remedy to liberate myself from the clutches of Narcissism.

While it may not represent absolute liberation, it is imperative to acknowledge that this is so due to the omnipresence and enduring influence of narcissism. An individual's resolve lies in establishing and upholding a personal obligation to oneself upon the definitive realization that one will no longer surrender their authority or allow the influence of a narcissist or any other individual to govern their actions.

A compassionate and empathetic person is invariably susceptible to being preyed upon by individuals with narcissistic tendencies; such is the nature of the situation. It is crucial to note that once you acquire expertise in the matter, you will have the ability to detect the indications and patterns well in advance of experiencing negative consequences. Now, you have gained an advantage over them and will implement proactive measures to shield yourself from their manipulative strategies. As you reclaim your power, the sense of victimhood will progressively diminish.

In order to achieve the desired outcome of a pursuit, it is imperative to consciously devote a substantial effort towards it. It is imperative that you engage in reading, deliberate upon the material, reflect upon its contents, and allot yourself the necessary time to comprehensively grasp its meaning. According to a wise individual, one should permit knowledge to percolate from the mind, gradually embracing wisdom until one confidently seizes it and proclaims, 'Let us embark on this journey together.'

Notice that wherever you venture, individuals frequently discuss God in relation to an entity separate from the individual. Additionally, they discuss His presence within. The majority possess the ability to comprehend the observable realities pertaining to a superior and elevated intellect in operation. However, when it comes to comprehending the intellect inherent in it, it eludes us as an abstract concept.

If an individual elucidates our existence through the lens of a mathematical equation, positing that we are integral components of a larger entity, a newfound coherence can be discerned. Consider the notion that each individual, be it Einstein, Abraham Lincoln, or Barack Obama, is partaking in predetermined roles ordained by a divine entity known as God. I understand your point, however, what about individuals who engage in malevolent actions? This becomes unclear once more due to the incomprehensibility of why a virtuous being would partake in such heinous acts.

Allow us to revert the focus of this situation to the mistreatment of a person with narcissistic tendencies. Imagine if I were to suggest to you that notwithstanding the anguish and dreadful ordeal you have endured or may presently be enduring, your life following an encounter with a narcissist has the potential to improve by a magnitude of ten compared to the past. If you were previously unaware of your purpose, it is evident that matters are now becoming more lucid. You are capable of enhancing your mental focus. This fosters personal growth, encourages increased support for others, and endeavors to protect individuals from enduring similarly distressing circumstances.

Consequently, it can be inferred that you are currently in a state of disrepair. You harbor the belief that you have lost your capacity to place trust in others.

You will discover an innate resilience that was previously unknown to you.

Due to the actions of this detestable individual, whose intentions were malevolent, the inherent determination within you has managed to utilize it for benevolent purposes. The malevolent individual inadvertently facilitated the realization of your potential for greatness.

When engaged in the act of reading, it is advised to adopt a deliberate and contemplative approach, striving to attentively perceive and evaluate any content that resonates with one's personal beliefs or experiences. Subsequently, engage in thoughtful reflection, repeatedly analyzing it mentally, subsequently record your thoughts, and permit them to flow gradually.

As you prepare to retire for the night, reflect upon this truth, and drift into slumber with a renewed state of mind. Understanding that while you are peacefully resting, your life is steadily improving.

Develop a coherent strategy for your recuperation

While perusing this literary material, kindly take note of any deficiencies you happen to discern within your own character and subsequently devise a strategy to rectify them. It is imperative that you avoid excessively exerting yourself. Engaging in a brief five-minute concentration exercise every other day is more effective than compelling oneself to endure lengthy periods of uninterrupted sitting.

One possible alternative in a more formal tone could be: "A potential formulation for your list might be as follows: identification of his manipulative behavior."

His devious tactics: he telephones to inform me of his potential visit in the near future. It is customary for him to engage in such activities, although his attendance is infrequent.

Objective: to regulate my actions.

My usual course of action entails waiting in a state of apprehension, fully aware of the considerable likelihood that his arrival will not come to fruition. He refuses to offer an apology and instead fabricates dishonest explanations.

Healthy And Unhealthy Narcissism

There exists a correlation between a state of well-being characterized by a positive sense of self-importance and a healthy form of narcissism, although it ought to be clarified that they are distinct concepts. The experience entails deriving pleasure from one's physical attractiveness, the functioning of one's intellect, and the successful accomplishment of a challenging task executed with precision. It is a profound and exhilarating sense of self-satisfaction. Whilst the fleeting nature of beneficial self-admiration cannot be denied, it remains an influential and long-lasting phenomenon.

The Stages of Narcissistic Behavior in the Development of Childhood

At a certain stage in their development, it is generally expected that children will primarily focus on their own needs and interests. The initial phase of narcissistic development commences around the age of two, coinciding with the emergence of verbal language in children. During this phase, children typically develop a vocabulary that includes self-referential pronouns such as "I," "my," and "no." This coincides with a tendency to exhibit egocentric behavior, wherein their perspective is centered solely on themselves, often disregarding the needs and desires of others.

Assuming development proceeds in a typical manner, the child acquires knowledge through direct engagement with parents, peers, and educators, thereby recognizing that individuals around them possess their own aspirations and preferences. Egocentrism diminishes, and the adolescent develops a sense of empathy towards others.

Adults possess the capacity to foster a state of healthy self-importance, even if it no longer hinges on assuming the role of the focal point in the world. It entails experiencing an overwhelming sense of elation and contentment derived from one's personal accomplishments and influential contributions to society.

Healthy self-regard is of utmost importance for a variety of reasons, primarily because it can serve as a valuable asset during challenging situations, enabling one to derive profound satisfaction from their own abilities and qualities. For instance, in the event that an individual is capable of deriving narcissistic gratification from effectively completing arduous tasks, it may serve as a source of endurance during times of discouragement and setback, thereby mitigating the risk of experiencing burnout.

Certain individuals fail to cultivate a robust sense of self-regard due to their apprehension regarding potential envy from others. When a young individual becomes aware that they may face penalties or adverse treatment for attaining success, that child will adopt a tendency to withhold or downplay their exceptional abilities, perhaps even obscuring them from their own awareness.

If you identify with this description, endeavor to perceive your healthy narcissism in the light of gratitude for the blessings and accomplishments you possess. Expressing gratitude for your inherent abilities might enable you to value them without excessive arrogance.

ATTRIBUTES OF WELL-BALANCED NARCISSISM (As Per Kohut)

The ability to understand and embrace the admiration of others.

A robust sense of personal worth and esteem.

A strong sense of self-worth and accomplishment

A comprehension of the requirements and the ability to cultivate empathy towards others.

Emotional toughness

Self-esteem and respect

Authenticity

The ability to maintain self-approval while accepting the disapproval of others.

The ability to possess aspirations, visions, aspirations, and confidence in one's capability to make a decision that will positively impact one's life.

How can we cultivate a constructive form of self-regard?

One dedicates a greater portion of time to themselves than to any other individual. Acquire the knowledge of self-compassion, boundaries, and self-esteem.

We are social beings. Utilize the knowledge acquired earlier to individuals in your vicinity.

Empathy development, proactive empathy (philanthropy), and communal empathy (community engagement).

Assure yourself. Engage in introspection to discern the factors that instill a sense of self-assurance within you.

Embark on the path to achieve your objectives while simultaneously recognizing your aptitudes and imperfections.

Assist others. Construct them. Encourage.

Learn to have faith. Understand how to forgive.

Foster your individuality instead of conforming to societal expectations.

Direct your attention to your internal state.

Could you please provide an explanation of unhealthy narcissism?

People who exhibit unhealthy levels of narcissism lack the ability to establish reciprocal connections or engage in partnerships. They will conduct their actions through either persistent devaluation of others or by self-elevation at the expense of those in their vicinity. In the former situation, they must seek out an individual whom they can idealize and establish a strong connection with, while in the latter, they necessitate the admiration and reverence of others. In either situation, the narcissist engages in the mistreatment of individuals prior to forsaking them, proceeding to target the next victim without displaying any signs of remorse.

AN OVERVIEW OF TYPICAL NARCISSISM (NN) AND THE DIAGNOSIS OF NARCISSISTIC PERSONALITY DISORDER (NPD)

Numerous individuals possess minor narcissistic inclinations within their character traits. It is a natural response to experience a sense of self-satisfaction or increased self-esteem when accomplishing significant achievements or presenting oneself in an aesthetically appealing manner. Moreover, such sentiments of pride can engender a heightened sense of individualism. However, having such feelings on occasion does not make you a narcissist.

Genuine narcissists exhibit dominant narcissistic traits that permeate their personalities and govern their lives. The condition exerts influence over various aspects of their life, encompassing their professional endeavors, interpersonal relationships, and romantic involvements. Narcissistic Personality Disorder, akin to numerous other personality disorders, presents a formidable challenge in terms of treatment. Individuals afflicted with Narcissistic Personality Disorder (NPD) exhibit an inflated perception of their own significance. They exhibit a notable absence of empathy and interest in the perspectives of others, yet concurrently possess a strong yearning for external validation and recognition. Hence, even if they display disinterest towards others, they actively pursue social interactions in order to obtain the attention they perceive as their rightful due.

Narcissistic Personality Disorder (NPD) is distinguished by a vulnerable, rigid, and impractical perception of oneself. Individuals diagnosed with Narcissistic

Personality Disorder (NPD) are compelled to uphold their fragile sense of self-worth by harboring a deep-seated conviction in their exceptionalism. This phenomenon serves as the fundamental cause behind the development of numerous behavioral patterns exhibited by individuals. This is the reason why individuals with NPD exhibit emotional reactions even towards the most insignificant forms of criticism, as an illustrative instance. This is precisely why their endeavors are characterized by a strong determination to obtain recognition and esteem. Their identity becomes highly vulnerable in its absence.

With regard to psychology, it should be noted that narcissism and authentic self-compassion are not synonymous. Individuals afflicted with narcissistic personality disorder (NPD) are purportedly deeply enamored with an idealized and inflated perception of their own being.

Narcissistic personality disorder is typified by a consistent display of egocentric, haughty cognition and conduct, a deficiency in empathy and concern for others, and an all-consuming longing for admiration. Narcissistic Personality Disorder individuals are frequently perceived by others as possessing traits such as arrogance, manipulation, egocentrism, pretentiousness, and a disposition towards making excessive demands. This cognitive and behavioral pattern manifests itself across various domains of the narcissist's existence, encompassing professional endeavors, friendships, familial interactions, and personal relationships alike.

Individuals diagnosed with narcissistic personality disorder exhibit a notable resistance towards altering their patterns of behavior, regardless of the adversities it may be causing them. They exhibit a tendency to attribute blame to others. Additionally, they display a considerable level of sensitivity and exhibit strong reactions towards even the slightest form of criticism, disagreements, or perceived slights, which they interpret as personal affronts. Individuals who reside in close proximity to a narcissistic individual often perceive it as a more convenient course of action to acquiesce to their requests in order to circumvent their aloofness and anger.

Nevertheless, through gaining a deeper understanding of narcissistic personality disorder, you will acquire the ability to identify narcissistic individuals within your surroundings, safeguard yourself against their manipulative tactics, and establish more robust personal boundaries.

HEALTHY (NN) VS. UNHEALTHY (NPD) NARCISSISM

The key differentiation between the two lies in the fact that NPD constitutes a protracted, enduring pattern of self-aggrandizing beliefs and behaviors. On occasions when individuals experience profound distress, it is not uncommon for them to exhibit a lack of consideration and self-centered behavior.

Self-esteem

Individuals diagnosed with Narcissistic Personality Disorder (NPD) exhibit markedly diminished levels of self-esteem. Others may perceive them to possess inflated self-importance, however, this is merely a facade concealing their underlying insecurities. Due to their diminished self-esteem, they possess a desire for continuous affirmation, even adulation, from others.

Individuals from the NN community exhibit elevated levels of self-confidence. They typically engage in endeavors that contribute to the welfare of their families, professional aspirations, and local communities, thereby imbuing their lives with a sense of meaning. The approval of others is indeed pleasant, however, it does not constitute a requisite for one's self-esteem.

Relationships with other people

Individuals diagnosed with narcissistic personality disorder tend to seek out individuals who can provide them with reassurance to mitigate their profound feelings of insecurity. They consistently strive to maintain a superior level of authority, status, and dominion over others. Their associations frequently revolve around the extent to which others can be of assistance to them or enhance their public image. It is highly unusual for them to retain someone once their services are no longer necessary to pursue their individual objectives. Individuals suffering from NPD engage in a pattern of orchestrating acceptance and rejection in order to manipulate their spouses, colleagues, and individuals they perceive as friends, as they seek a sense of security by maintaining control over their surroundings.

Individuals who possess NN exhibit a notable level of self-assurance. They need not adopt a sense of superiority in order to attain a feeling of self-sufficiency. Their motivation to connect with other individuals who share a similar drive stems from their genuine passion for their work, rather than any intention to take advantage of them. Their relationships are built upon the principle of parity and are characterized by an equitable exchange of resources and reciprocity. They develop enduring relationships of acceptance and support.

Empathy

Individuals diagnosed with Narcissistic Personality Disorder may exhibit acts of compassion under the condition that it fulfills their inherent need for interpersonal connection. Displaying compassionate behavior is perceived as a means for them to establish their reputation as an exemplary individual in the perception of others. If the objective is to shift focus from their own dilemmas, their empathy will only be transitory.

Individuals who possess NN are inclined towards assisting others. When they engage in conversations regarding their charitable endeavors, the primary objective is to garner increased assistance for individuals facing significant challenges. Their love is boundless, and their compassion knows no bounds.

The correlation between success and failure

Individuals diagnosed with Narcissistic Personality Disorder frequently engage in the amplification of their accomplishments and exhibit an inflated perception of their abilities. It is not infrequent for them to lay claim to the achievements of others. If individuals fail to impress through their own accomplishments, they will resort to highlighting the shortcomings or failures of others in order to create a façade of excellence. Predictably, individuals exhibit reluctance to openly address their inadequacies or mistakes due to concerns about adversely influencing others' perceptions of them.

When individuals possessing NN engage in dialogue concerning an achievement, they do so with utmost veracity, accompanied by justified and modest satisfaction. Contrary to individuals with Narcissistic Personality Disorder (NPD), they are not required to gauge their accomplishments in relation to those of others. They are prepared to acknowledge and attribute credit to others. Individuals who possess NN demonstrate a proclivity for being candid and forthright in acknowledging their errors and shortcomings. They acknowledge the inherent nature of making mistakes and understand that engaging in open dialogue about their shortcomings does not diminish their worth.

Reaction to criticism

Individuals with Narcissistic Personality Disorder exhibit a heightened sensitivity to criticism and tend to respond in an exaggerated manner to perceived insults, whether real or imagined. They exhibit a persistent reluctance to acknowledge accountability for unfavorable decisions or objectionable actions. When faced with any mistake or offense, they promptly shift the blame onto another individual, absolving themselves of accountability. Should that strategy prove unsuccessful, they will assert that external coercion compelled their actions.

Individuals with NN may also exhibit a tendency to be averse to conflict or disapproval, thereby seeking to evade these situations whenever feasible. Upon contemplation, individuals have the capacity to partake in productive dialogue amidst unfavorable circumstances. They willingly assume accountability for their mistakes and are enthusiastic about modifying their perspectives and behaviors. They possess the ability to express regret to others without experiencing unwarranted feelings of inferiority.

Subsequent to bidding adieu to my family, I eagerly embarked upon an extensive air travel spanning twenty-three hours, bound for North America. I possessed no inkling about the nature of my forthcoming experiences. My understanding was limited to the fact that the opportunity I had longed for, for a period exceeding two years, was now on the verge of becoming a tangible possibility.

I inadvertently succumbed to slumber, as was my customary practice during lengthy aerial journeys, only to awaken abruptly due to an overwhelming emetic sensation. I proceeded to the lavatory aboard the aircraft and expeditiously attended to my personal needs, mindful of the presence of other passengers waiting in queue. It marked the initial occurrence of three visits to the lavatory prior to the culmination of that flight.

Upon our arrival at Pearson International Airport, I experienced severe dehydration and disorientation, rendering me almost incapable of standing. However, I persevered and endured an additional six-hour wait at the airport to obtain my study permits prior to proceeding to my designated lodging.

The demeanor of my Uber driver appeared rather aloof during the entire 45-minute ride, displaying minimal engagement in response to my attempts at casual conversation. I detected an implicit undertone of 'why didn't you choose to remain in your country of origin?' Could it be that the cause of this was solely attributed to my perception? However, in order to maximize my time effectively, I directed my attention out the window, absorbing the breathtaking scenery of the countryside that would serve as my residence for the upcoming year.

Upon arriving at the Inn, where I had previously made reservations for a duration of two nights, the chauffeur proceeded to unload my luggage without any delay. Regrettably, I was unable to utter a single word or seek assistance in opening the reception door before he hastily deposited all of my belongings at the entrance and swiftly departed from the scene. In the frigid temperature, I surveyed my surroundings in search of someone who could potentially assist me with my burdensome luggage. Alas, there was an absence of any individuals to offer aid. Upon arrival in Canada, I silently acknowledged the welcoming atmosphere while struggling to pull my weighty luggage through the wintry conditions towards the accommodations reserved for me and my fellow Indian student, where we were to stay for the duration of the next two nights.

After a restful period of two days and having enjoyed my inaugural Canadian meal, I was prepared to embark on the quest for more enduring lodging options. I conducted an online search to locate the nearest taxi service and, after an hour had passed, a taxi arrived at my location to transport me to my initial destination.

The taxi driver was an attractive individual of Iranian descent with a fiery mane of ginger hair, who went by the name of Sam. He was a recent recipient of a degree, in his mid-20s, and had recently acquired his permanent residency. Sam quickly established himself as my frequent chauffeur, demonstrating a heightened understanding of my predicament as a foreigner seeking appropriate lodging.

Sam kindly extended his assistance during his non-working hours, acknowledging my lack of acquaintances and unfamiliarity with the surroundings in Oshawa, the city where my college was situated. He had a strong resolve to assist me in getting adjusted before the commencement of school. He provided transportation to a bank and Service Canada for the purpose of depositing the funds I had brought and completing the registration process for obtaining a social insurance number.

After the conclusion of my tenure at the college-provided accommodations, Sam kindly offered to transport me to the Airbnb where I would temporarily lodge until I had arranged for a more enduring living arrangement.

I was received graciously by an amiable Indian couple and their two offspring. That occurred during the evening of New Year's Eve, a time at which all individuals had already made arrangements. The Indian couple graciously extended their hospitality by presenting me with a bottle of red wine prior to embarking on the celebrations.

Later in the day, Sam phoned me to inquire about my well-being and informed me of his intention to visit his relatives. I expressed my gratitude to him for his invaluable assistance and extended my heartfelt wishes for a joyous New Year. He would subsequently notify me, after a span of one week, that he would be relocating to Milton with the purpose of commencing a new employment opportunity. Additionally, he kindly requested that I should not hesitate to reach out to him in the event that I required any further assistance or information to facilitate my own stay. I expressed my gratitude to the Almighty for bringing Sam into my life during those initial days. I truly cannot fathom the immense challenges I would have faced without his invaluable assistance.

While the rest of the individuals were engaged in New Year's Eve festivities, I took the opportunity to settle down, positioning myself in front of the television. Subsequently, I accessed the Netflix streaming service and commenced viewing one of my preferred television series. I had the auditory experience of fireworks and the elevated excitement displayed by individuals partaking in the festivities I was appreciative to, at the very least, have a accommodation where I could rest my head as I commenced this new undertaking.

Academic activities recommenced on January sixth at the college. The initial course proved beneficial as it afforded me the opportunity to acquaint myself with fellow students hailing from various countries. We engaged in a discussion pertaining to the comparable difficulties encountered in terms of lodging and transportation. I discovered that students were granted complimentary access to public transportation upon presentation of their student identification. This information was truly invigorating to my senses, given that my actions upon arrival were solely oriented towards extravagant expenditure.

A few days later, I would additionally transition into lodging that is conveniently situated directly across from the college. Although the cost was somewhat high, considering the limited time available, it was the most optimal choice I could have made.

After a span of two weeks, I had started to acclimate to my unfamiliar surroundings in a foreign nation, in which I had virtually no acquaintances. Fortunately, I was fortunate enough to receive generous assistance from benevolent individuals who provided me with substantial aid during this situation. Additionally, when it came time to relocate my belongings to my lodging, my newfound classmates graciously extended their support.

My initial intention was to acclimate myself to the demands of my academic schedule before embarking on a job search - an endeavor that was imperative given my rapidly depleting financial resources and lack of income. Additionally, as a person with religious beliefs, I sought a place of worship and thus conducted an online search for Nigerian churches located in Oshawa, resulting in the discovery of two options. I chose the option in closer proximity to my lodging, unaware at the time that I would ultimately navigate my way to the alternative.

Additionally, I had a strong desire for Nigerian cuisine, yet was oblivious regarding its availability. I had anticipated encountering fellow

Nigerians who could kindly guide me to an establishment where I could procure authentic Nigerian cuisine. I was unaccustomed to burgers and wraps that lacked substantial levels of seasoning. Indeed, we Nigerians have earned a prominent reputation for our affinity towards cuisine endowed with vibrant and fiery flavors.

After a period of two months, I had established a more enduring living arrangement, adjusted to my academic schedule, formed connections with a few individuals who had recently arrived in Canada, discovered a place of worship, and secured employment commencing in early March. Upon reflection, I found it quite impressive for an individual unfamiliar with the surroundings.

My recently acquired residence is a townhouse with five bedrooms, conveniently situated directly across from the college. There were a total of four individuals present, and three among us were international students. The teenage Canadian Michelle, who constituted the fourth individual, exuded an aesthetic characterized by Gothic elements, such as her black lipstick, spiky black hair, and similar attributes. I had solely encountered this particular lifestyle through televised portrayals, and the prospect of residing alongside someone who leads such a life appeared intriguing.

The sole disadvantage was her preference for being awake during nocturnal hours. She would engage in extended periods of rest or remain indoors throughout the day, while remaining awake during nighttime hours. The remainder of our group consisted of students who typically had demanding schedules due to their scholastic and professional commitments. However, Michelle would remain awake throughout the night indulging in drinking, preparing meals, and engaging in animated conversations with her boyfriend, oblivious to the slumber of the rest of our group. Or tried to sleep.

This eventually posed a challenge as her volume progressively increased during the nights, and she persistently ran the laundry throughout the nighttime hours, creating an environment akin to a commercial launderette. It proved to be quite challenging for me, as my room happened to be located directly beneath the laundry machine, and unfortunately, I have a tendency to be easily awakened. The situation quickly progressed from evenings filled with disruptive noise to intense verbal altercations between her and her boyfriend, to instances where the fire alarm was triggered multiple times, and to instances of our belongings stored in the refrigerator disappearing. As one can ascertain, this began instilling a sense of discomfort in the remainder of our group. Therefore, we determined to engage in a conversation with her.

We engaged in a conversation with her, yet regrettably, she failed to acknowledge the gravity of the situation. As matters escalated beyond a manageable state, it became necessary for us to escalate the matter to the attention of the management. Subsequently, they reached a consensus and established a designated timeframe for laundering, with the expectation that it would offer assistance. It indeed had an impact, albeit only for a duration of approximately one week. Subsequently, the situation deteriorated further. The college physician had made a diagnosis of a sleep disorder at that juncture. Due to the disruptive noises at night, I found myself unable to sleep, resulting in excessive compensatory sleep during the day and subsequent tardiness in attending my classes.

Due to the management's inability to implement any further immediate modifications, my sole recourse was to seek an alternative lodging. I conducted a thorough examination of various options and ultimately secured accommodation in close proximity to the college. I made the decision to accept the accommodation without having had the opportunity to meet my prospective housemate. At that juncture, I was willing to undertake any measure to obtain a restful night's sleep.

During the month of February, reports regarding the Corona Virus came to light, although the perception of this illness remained somewhat remote, being likened to a form of influenza. However, the influenza outbreak began causing significant fatalities and was no longer feasible to neglect. As a result, the World Health Organization commenced urging individuals worldwide to acknowledge its severity. To such an extent, that come March 2020, the

Canadian authorities issued a formal directive for individuals to remain at their residences, pending a more comprehensive understanding of the situation and effective measures to mitigate the spread of infection.

Consequently, establishments and enterprises that drew substantial crowds of people, such as educational institutions, theaters, recreational areas, seashores, conventions, musical performances, drinking establishments, dining establishments, commercial complexes, and similar venues, were compelled to cease operations, necessitating the transition of many enterprises to virtual platforms. The global health crisis would demonstrate positive outcomes for e-commerce enterprises and on-demand streaming services such as Netflix and Prime Video. These were primarily the sole sources of amusement that individuals relied upon to maintain their sanity while confined indoors.

Upon arriving at my recently acquired residence, I had the opportunity to encounter the additional resident who happens to be a female student pursuing a degree in legal administration. This fortuitous meeting coincided with my first day of occupancy. The third occupant of the house happened to be the son of the homeowners, who works in the field of mortuary science. Due to the increased workload at the morgues amid the COVID-19 situation, he consistently remained dedicated to his work. This circumstance resulted in the young female housemate and myself being predominantly at home on days when I was not engaged in work-related activities.

After a lapse of seven days since my arrival, I started to discern that a romantic affiliation existed between the other two individuals. After a scant fortnight of residing there, I ascertained that she exhibited a profound territorial disposition, frequently reorganizing or modifying the arrangement of my belongings in communal areas such as the kitchen and washroom to accommodate her personal preferences. On certain occasions, she would inadvertently combine perishable food items in close proximity, resulting in their subsequent spoilage.

On a certain occasion, I was in the process of heating up a meal for consumption when she abruptly entered the kitchen and expressed her disdain for the unpleasant odor emanating from my food. I frequently pondered whether she, should she have resided with individuals of indigenous heritage renowned for their creation of dishes imbued with intense flavors, would have been inclined to provide them with feedback regarding what she perceived as disagreeable olfactory qualities in their cuisine. This phenomenon may elucidate the inclination of individuals from the same cultural background to coalesce and inhabit shared communities.

Addressing Traumatic Brain Injuries And Facilitating Recovery

As previously mentioned, narcissistic abuse possesses the capacity to induce physical alterations in the structure of the human brain. In the absence of restoration of this change and subsequent normalization of brain function, it will impede your ability to progress and move forward in your life. This may result in the experience of C-PTSD symptoms. Let us now examine several strategies that can facilitate the process of brain healing.

Meditation

The allocation of time for meditation may serve to hinder its practice. You endeavor to allocate every possible opportunity to find time, but the demands of daily existence impede your efforts. It is simply challenging to allocate a single hour for oneself.

Although there are advantages to engaging in prolonged meditation, it is possible to enhance cognitive function by dedicating just a few minutes per day to this practice. Mindfulness meditation, in particular, has the potential to enhance both the mental and physical well-being of individuals. It aids in the reduction of blood pressure, cortisol levels, and stress levels.

These recommendations can assist you in achieving a state of mental tranquility even during periods of utmost busyness.

Method of execution:

Direct your attention towards your breath, observing the movement of your abdomen and chest as you engage in the act of inhaling and exhaling.

Conduct a thorough examination of the body, specifically focusing on identifying regions where tension is present.

Engage in cognitive examination: Encourage your mind to decelerate and assess your thoughts impartially without imposing judgment upon them.

Familiarize yourself with your emotions: Feelings are transient, and it is within your discretion to determine your desired reaction.

Carefully observe: Select an item and fix your gaze upon it, such as a flickering candle or a tree branch swaying in the wind.

Recite: Engage in the act of mentally uttering your chosen mantra or a personal affirmation. Repeat this three times.

Tactile Sensation: The majority of religious practices incorporate the utilization of beads or similar objects to track the quantity of prayers recited, safeguarding against drowsiness.

When to Meditate:

Harness your determination: Employ the presence of stop signs and traffic signs as an opportunity to pause and refresh.

Utilize intermittent pauses during meetings to maintain mental engagement, treating it with the same conscious attentiveness as you would your mobile device.

Enhance physical training: Monitor your mental state during the process of strengthening your physique. Engage in contemplative practices such as swimming or utilizing a treadmill for introspection.

Establish communication with your counterpart: Engage in a social outing with your partner or companion. Engage in joint morning and evening meditation sessions.

Nurture a connection with your children: Mindfulness exercises prove to be highly beneficial for the well-being of children. Engage in mental imagery, vocal exercises, or yoga postures.

Formation: Our daily existence can be punctuated by queues. On your next occasion of queuing at the store, engaging in meditation will effectively assist in utilizing the waiting period.

Do not engage with advertisements: If you find commercials undesirable, utilize the mute button and appreciate the tranquility.

Practice conscious eating: When faced with a challenging day, do you tend to gravitate towards readily available sugary treats or alcoholic beverages?

Engage in a brief session of meditation to alleviate distress.

Meditation constitutes the most frequently employed therapeutic modality in my personal healing regimen. Ensuring that I allocated time for this activity posed the greatest challenge; nevertheless, upon recognizing the consequential positive effects, I prioritized its inclusion in my schedule.

Cognitive Behavioral Therapy

Presented herewith are a compilation of prevalent cognitive behavioral therapy exercises that serve as efficacious tools to support diverse forms of treatment scenarios:

- Cognitive Reorganization
- Cognitive Reconfiguration
- Cognitive Restructuration

This exercise has been specifically developed to facilitate the evaluation of cognitive patterns that are detrimental. It facilitates the generation of novel responses to challenging situations. This necessitates maintaining a comprehensive log of your cognitive processes, facilitating the identification of maladaptive automatic thoughts and subsequent development of alternative responses. This task can be accomplished either with the assistance of a licensed therapist or independently.

• Organization of Activities

This exercise will facilitate the undertaking of actions that are not typically within your usual repertoire. This intervention prompts individuals to engage in behaviors that they would not typically partake in, thereby enabling them to allocate dedicated time for said behaviors. It is commonly employed for the treatment of depression and serves as a means to reintegrate gratifying activities into one's daily regimen. It is advisable to embark upon this endeavor under the supervision of a therapist, while the execution of the behavior is ultimately conducted independently.

- Systematic Desensitization

This exercise aims to alleviate fear and anxiety through exposure to activities that elicit apprehension. This treatment modality offers the highest degree of efficacy for addressing the majority of psychological concerns. The theory pertains to the avoidance of feared stimuli, which consequently leads to heightened levels of anxiety and fear. By consistently engaging in activities or situations that you typically avoid, you will experience a perpetuated decrease in anxiety. It is advisable to initially engage the services of a therapist for this task.

• Gradual Approach • Incremental Refinement • Iterative Progress • Steady Advancement

This is an exercise designed to assist you in addressing challenging objectives or goals that may feel overwhelming. By dividing complex tasks into smaller, manageable steps or engaging in related tasks that pose less difficulty, one can cultivate the necessary expertise to ultimately attain mastery in the desired skill. This task can be accomplished independently.

• Skill Development Program • Training in Skills Enhancement • Professional Skill Building Course • Skill Enhancement Training Session

This is an activity designed to address deficiencies in skills and employs techniques such as role-playing, direct instruction, and modeling in order to achieve improvement. The prevailing topics include training in communication, training in assertiveness, and training in social skills. This is commonly undertaken in the presence of a therapist or within the framework of group therapy.

• Resolving Issues • Troubleshooting • Finding Solutions • Analyzing and Resolving Problems • Addressing Challenges • Mitigating Obstacles • Overcoming Difficulties • Resolving Complications

This exercise facilitates individuals to actively engage in the process of identifying and resolving their own challenges. Continuously experiencing letdowns or persistent emotional difficulties may ensue when one assumes a passive stance in the face of challenging issues. By acquiring the skill of problem-solving, one can restore authority and render challenging circumstances less arduous. This task can be accomplished independently, with the guidance of a qualified therapist, or as part of a group therapy setting.

Chapter 2. Several Types Of Narcissists

Narcissists, despite displaying considerable similarities amongst themselves, can often be classified into one of three distinct categories. They can manifest in a conspicuous, clandestine, or venomous manner. These individuals, characterized by their egocentric tendencies, indeed adhere to the criteria of an egotist, albeit manifesting distinct codes of personal conduct. The transparent individuals are mostly highly distinguished, whereas the covert individuals have chosen to maintain an air of secrecy regarding their self-centered tendencies. The exceptionally malevolent narcissists constitute the minority whose primary intent is to inflict maximum pain and suffering upon individuals in order to cause harm. Gaining insight into the distinct manifestations of egocentric behavior can facilitate the identification of individuals who possess self-centered tendencies, as one would be capable of observing specific patterns of personal conduct.

You will acquire a broadened breadth of understanding regarding the manner in which egotists may manifest themselves, enabling you to be better equipped in handling their presence.

The Covert Narcissist

Covert individuals, occasionally referred to as individuals with a lack of strong self-esteem, exhibit a penchant for maintaining secrecy surrounding their methods of control. They often seek refuge behind the guise of casualty, particularly due to their heightened sensitivity towards rejection or feelings of abandonment. They leverage their sense of apprehension regarding being dismissed as a driving force to manipulate others into maintaining close proximity, and their most effective strategy for retaining those around them involves feigning a greater need for assistance and support than they actually require. People are generally more inclined to assist individuals who have been harmed or misled, thus explaining the secretive egotist's tendency to adopt a victim mentality.

The covert narcissist frequently oscillates between feelings of insufficiency and superiority, depending on recent events. In moments of averageness, they actively seek self-centered gratification, assuming the role of a victim in order to fulfill their wants or desires. Whenever individuals have been recipients of someone else's thoughtfulness, they can subsequently incline back towards experiencing a sense of dominance, as their egos have recently been bolstered by their own acts of assistance.

Covert individuals with an inflated sense of self often exhibit strong adherence to traditional values and beliefs. They exhibit poor adaptability to unexpected situations, and in instances of being deprived of their desired objectives, they frequently respond with explosive behavior, even though they commonly present themselves as tranquil, tentative individuals. Clearly, when provoked, the concealed egotist exhibits an impressive level of potency and can manifest notably aggressive and formidable behavior when confronted. They may assume the guise of individuals facing similar challenges, yet they struggle to maintain this façade when overwhelmed, henceforth surrendering their vulnerable, unrefined, authentic nature to scrutiny.

Generally, following the evaluation, the covert narcissist initiates a series of suppressed hostility attempts to maintain their desired persona. Kindly ensure that the individual assuming the undercover identity maintains this façade of self-importance. As an illustration, consider the scenario where you have a discreetly self-absorbed associate who regularly arrives home from work late, thus causing you to frantically rush in order to arrive at your workplace punctually, as she neglects to assist you with childcare responsibilities. Given the circumstances, it would be appropriate to advise her that it would be advisable for her to contact you in the event that she anticipates being delayed, in order for you to make necessary adjustments and arrange for alternative arrangements if necessary. Your self-absorbed significant other may become emotional, expressing disappointment in your lack of trust in her and emphasizing her earnest efforts for the betterment of the family. She becomes so deeply engrossed in her professional endeavors and striving for financial gains that she inadvertently overlooks and fails to recognize her potential as a reliable and capable companion.

Abruptly, the burden is shifted onto your shoulders. There are two options remaining: either you affirmatively assure her of her competency, thus endorsing her casual mindset, or you refrain from acknowledging it, risking her potential transition into a self-centered fury. Both options are equally unappealing for you, much like dealing with a narcissistic individual.

The primary strategic maneuver is to abstain from participating altogether.

In the end, the enigmatic narcissist possesses an inherent fragility and lack of confidence. She excessively worries about her indecisiveness to the extent that she claims not to exist. This is the fabricated persona that she constructs, deceiving herself and others. She is essentially compensating excessively for her limitations, creating an impression that leans towards pretentiousness in order to project a greater sense of self-confidence than she genuinely possesses.

She yearns for connections with others, yet she struggles to create meaningful ones due to her lack of empathy, while her self-worth becomes entangled with the validation received from others. She seeks validation and a sense of importance from others in order to boost her self-assurance, which is why she pretends to be someone else. She endeavours to foster interpersonal harmony, drawing upon her persuasion techniques discretely, in order to garner affections from others.

Usually, the individual assuming an incognito egotist role is the result of a childhood trauma that left her feeling abandoned or ignored. Through creating a persona of perfection, she is able to deny that the abuse, neglect, abandonment, or any other harm she experienced was her fault, and she can distance herself from the consequences of these traumas.

In the end, although the ostentatious narcissist seeks to be the center of attention and regarded as superior to everyone else, achieving power and recognition, the objectives of the feeble egotist are unquestionably more reasonable. She should possess exceptional abilities in any position she undertakes and be highly esteemed by her peers. She does not require an authoritative skill in order to be acknowledged for the effort she puts into her work. She should be regarded as an exceptional mother, spouse, companion, or valuable member of the community rather than being in a position of power. She will undertake the requisite measures to attain that position and conduct herself in ways that might not be perceived as egoistic, particularly if others are able to observe it. She will exercise a generous approach, nevertheless, this generosity should be practiced when others are in a state of disarray. She will demonstrate compassion and make sincere efforts to establish and nurture friendships, yet her lack of empathy for others, coupled with her persistent attempts to put herself at the forefront, will make maintaining relationships difficult.

What Is The Manifestation Of Narcissistic Traits?

The predominant origin of narcissism often cited pertains to individuals' significant others, such as their spouse or romantic partner. Nevertheless, the most detrimentally influential source stems from the familial milieu. Scientific inquiry and empirical knowledge have revealed that individuals raised within narcissistic family environments encounter considerable difficulty in discerning and addressing the challenges they encounter, as the prevalence of denial is starkly evident within their familial systems.

What are the prevailing family dynamics that arise in the presence of a narcissistic individual?
If the individual within the family unit displaying narcissistic traits happens to

be your parent, it is highly probable that they shall experience a profound sense of emptiness, perceiving themselves as flawed and insufficient. Furthermore, it is quite plausible that they may also grapple with feelings of depression and anxiety. An adult displaying narcissistic traits typically lacks understanding regarding the development of their personality.

As a consequence, the children are correspondingly more prone to the manifestation of conditions such as depression and anxiety. It is a frequent occurrence for individuals to seek treatment at a later stage in their lives in order to address their relationship difficulties or emotional symptoms. Nevertheless, they often fail to exhibit an understanding of the underlying etiology of their cognitive ailments. A family comprising one or more parents displaying narcissistic traits inevitably conceals a deep-seated anguish. These families adhere to a set of implicit guidelines. The children acquire the knowledge to adhere to those regulations, yet they fail to grasp their essence and perpetually experience distress due to them. These tacit rules present an impediment to their capacity for emotional connection with their parents. The children ultimately experience a sense of invisibility and become overlooked. Regrettably, the narcissistic parent will exploit these unspoken regulations to infringe upon their children's boundaries and exploit them when they deem it necessary.

In the following subsection, we shall examine the characteristics exhibited by a family affected by narcissism. This could potentially be beneficial if you are currently experiencing narcissistic mistreatment from a familial source. It is important to bear in mind that each family is unique, and dysfunction can vary along a spectrum based on the extent of narcissistic traits exhibited by the adults involved.

Lack of boundaries

There are few limitations or constraints present in a familial unit characterized by narcissism. The emotions of children are deemed insignificant. Emotional boundaries are consistently disregarded, physical boundaries are not maintained, and even personal journals are intruded upon. In the context of a narcissistic family, individuals are deprived of their inherent entitlement to personal privacy.

Harmful messages

Narcissistic parents consistently communicate explicit and implicit messages to their children, leading to the internalization of such messages. Typically, these messages revolve around the notions of inadequacy, insufficiency, or assessment solely based on actions rather than inherent identity. Consequently, children engage in exhaustive efforts to cater to the needs and expectations of the narcissistic parent.

Obvious/covert dysfunction

Typically, in the context of narcissistic families, the presence of dysfunctional dynamics is commonly veiled or overlooked by external observers. When the dysfunction occurs within abusive and violent households, the manifestations are typically conspicuous; however, this particular type is frequently clandestine when it pertains to psychological and emotional maltreatment. Despite the drama being kept private, its impact on the children remains substantial.

Feelings

Emotions within a household characterized by narcissism are generally avoided as topics of discussion and, when mentioned, are often rejected or dismissed. The parents consistently fail to educate their children on the appropriate methods of emotional processing or the importance of embracing emotions in a wholesome manner. Conversely, they are instructed to suppress their emotions entirely and frequently subjected to messaging that undermines the significance of their feelings. Narcissistic parents lack self-awareness regarding their own emotions, hence they tend to project these emotions onto their children. When the emotions of a narcissistic parent are suppressed, it gives rise to a dearth of sincerity and responsibility within the family unit, and in extreme instances, it may lead to the manifestation of psychological disorders. Insufficient instruction in the proper management of emotions often results in the manifestation of detrimental behavioral patterns.

Secrets

The concealed truth within a family with a narcissistic dynamic is that a parent who possesses narcissistic traits is incapable of adequately fulfilling the needs of their children. They might also engage in abusive behavior towards them. This behavior aligns with the prevailing pattern of narcissism within the family. The message conveyed to the children underscores the importance of maintaining secrecy regarding their troubles to external parties. The children are required to maintain the facade of their family being in good health and adhering to societal norms.

One parent exhibits narcissistic tendencies, while the other assumes the role of an orbiting parent.

The predominant form of interpersonal dynamics manifests wherein a single parent exhibits narcissistic tendencies, necessitating the other parent to devote themselves entirely to catering to their needs and sustaining the bond of marriage. This other parent typically possesses numerous commendable attributes that they can impart to their children. However, due to the majority of their time and energy being consumed by attending to the demands of their self-centered partner, they frequently neglect the welfare of their children. Regrettably, the children ultimately find themselves attempting to satisfy the demands of both parents in order to obtain the affection and care that they inherently require.

Ineffective communication

Regarding narcissistic families, triangulation is the prevailing mode of communication they employ. Instead of information being conveyed directly between individuals, the narcissistic parent typically employs the involvement of a third party in this communication, with the anticipation that it will eventually be relayed to their intended recipient. Each and every member of the family discusses and evaluates one another amongst themselves, yet they steadfastly refrain from engaging in direct confrontation. This form of communication engenders a passive-aggressive atmosphere that nurtures feelings of mistrust and tension. Direct communication usually occurs when someone is feeling anger.

Absence of a structured parental authority system

In typically functioning families, there exists a robust parental hierarchy wherein the parents assume the roles of mentorship, emotional support, and enlightenment for their children. This particular dynamic is not present within narcissistic families. As a result, it is the children who bear the responsibility of fulfilling the parents' needs.

Insufficient commitment to emotional accountability.

Due to the absence of empathy and unconditional love, narcissistic individuals are incapable of attaining a level of emotional comprehension and providing support to their offspring. They exhibit a propensity for criticism and judgment towards their children that surpasses their capacity for love and understanding. Hence, it is often observed that the offspring of such individuals make earnest efforts to fulfill their parents' expectations in order to gain acknowledgment and affection.

Siblings are pitted against each other.

In healthy family dynamics, it is highly encouraged for siblings to foster a close and affectionate relationship with one another. In households characterized by dysfunctional dynamics and the presence of a narcissistic individual, children frequently find themselves engaged in an unhealthy form of rivalry, orchestrated by the narcissist. There is an ongoing evaluation regarding which child exhibits superior qualities, while others may be deemed as lacking in some aspects. It is possible that there exists a discernible preference towards one of the children, alongside a tendency to attribute their parent's negative emotions onto the other children, effectively employing them as scapegoats. Typically, siblings raised within a narcissistic familial environment often lack emotional closeness with one another.

You consistently fall short of meeting the required standards.

The narcissistic parent often conveys the idea that their children fall short of expectations through various means. They have the option of communicating it verbally to their children or demonstrating it through their behavior. Generally, individuals with narcissistic tendencies exhibit conduct that is characterized by excessive self-promotion, hubris, and a deep sense of self-disparagement. Their deeply ingrained self-disdain and psychological state is the prevailing factor that is typically transmitted to their offspring.

Visual representation

In regards to a parent with narcissistic tendencies, their primary concern revolves around their public image and the perception others have of them. Their messaging to external audiences conveys the notion that their family perpetually remains superior, more expansive, and devoid of any predicaments. Furthermore, they compel their family members to don a facade of flawlessness. Offspring that are raised within this particular setting are consistently preoccupied with the opinions cast upon them by their relatives, neighbors, or acquaintances. They are apprehensive about the possibility that others may discern their true nature and perceive the internal disarray.

The Fundamental Element For Attaining Mastery

Have you laid your eyes upon a garden that has been forsaken? There will be the presence of weeds and sporadic growth throughout the area. It applies equally to your sense of self-worth. If one desires for it to thrive, it is imperative for it to be cultivated during one's formative years. Identify and unravel the various thoughts and emotions that contribute to the erosion of your self-esteem. This represents the initial stride towards actualizing your inherent value and embracing a genuine affection for oneself.

This chapter deals with building your self-esteem and practicing self-love because both of these actions will help you overcome codependency.

Engage in the Process of Internal Self-Reformation." "Facilitate the Reformation of Your Internal Critique." "Cultivate a Meticulous Approach to Re-Educating Your Inner Evaluator." "Undertake the Task of Internal Critic Refinement." "Embark on the Journey of Inner Critic Rehabilitation.

Every individual possesses an innate self-critical voice, and individuals who exhibit codependent tendencies possess an exceptionally influential one. This internal monologue incessantly highlights all of your deficiencies and errors. This vocal entity has the ability to function as a virtuous conscience at your discretion. However, it is often the case that one's inner critic has the potential to diminish their self-esteem through an excessive barrage of self-criticism. You may experience insecurity as your self-critic relentlessly undermines your ambition and erodes your confidence in various areas of life. Additionally, you may experience ambiguity, insufficiency, or a sense of inadequacy. Therefore, if you, in your capacity as a codependent individual, encounter challenges in striving towards your objectives, it is highly likely that your internal censor consistently exercises control and hinders your progress.

The intentions of your inner critic are never malevolent. It consistently endeavors to safeguard you from any adverse circumstances. However, there are instances when seeking protection may not be necessary, as it is important to venture out and experience the world firsthand. Should your inner critic be left unmanaged, it will inevitably transform into an unwavering purveyor of faults. Therefore, it is necessary to provide it with further education. The initial stage involves acknowledging your inner voice. To accomplish this, it is necessary to maintain a state of undisturbed tranquility, directing one's attention towards the prevailing thoughts. Commence the process of compiling a comprehensive inventory composed of any detrimental thoughts or self-deprecating tendencies that may be occupying your mind. Throughout the day, you may encounter your internal evaluator express various critiques. It is imperative that you remain vigilant and promptly record these criticisms as they arise within your thoughts.

Do not succumb to the influence of the 'instigator' within your mind.

Similar to the internal critic, each person possesses a cognitive entity referred to as the "Pusher," which consistently urges them to surpass their limits and undertake more responsibilities than they can feasibly manage. Therefore, in the event that the internal prompting from the 'Pusher' within your thoughts promotes increased productivity, it is not obligatory to heed its advice. There is no need to surrender oneself to servitude in order to accomplish one's list of tasks.

The 'Pusher' perpetually disrupts your inner tranquility. Even in moments of leisure, this persistent voice within you, referred to as the 'Pusher,' will compel you to address numerous outstanding matters within your life. The 'Pusher,' in conjunction with your internal critic, collaborates to bring forth unhappiness in your life. The sole means of liberating oneself from this mindset is to periodically embark on brief vacations. Monitor your anxiety levels and periodically pause to alleviate accumulated stress.

Accept Imperfection

As an individual with codependency tendencies, it is imperative to comprehend that the pursuit of perfectionism holds no true value, as every individual is innately flawed and imperfect. After comprehending this reality, the subsequent course of action involves embracing and cherishing your flaws. When an individual with codependency tendencies harbors the belief of their imperfections, it gives rise to feelings of shame, thereby initiating a process of accumulation within their cognitive processes. Over time, they develop an increasing apprehension of being rejected by those around them. Upon careful consideration, one will come to comprehend that perfectionism is solely motivated by feelings of shame. Individuals with a perfectionistic disposition often allocate their entirety of effort towards scrutinizing their deficiencies and errors. Deep within your innermost being, you harbor the belief that you are insufficient in various aspects of your existence.

Certain individuals gravitate towards perfectionism as a means of seeking respite from the myriad of difficulties encountered in their existence. Ultimately, this results in a state wherein one is incapable of completing any assigned tasks due to the fear of imperfection. The inner critic perpetually assesses your actions and impels you to fulfill the unattainable expectations and standards that you have devised within your cognition. Do you possess knowledge about the remedy for such behavior? Well, it is self-acceptance.

Once you embark upon the process of embracing and acknowledging your true self, a substantial portion of your troubles shall be alleviated.

Do not resort to making excuses

To cultivate a positive self-image, it is imperative to abstain from engaging in the practice of shifting responsibility and instead, carry oneself without making excuses. However, failure to do so will result in a permanent portrayal of yourself as the victim in all circumstances. You will also rely on others and their opinions of you in order to experience a sense of validation. Should you seek external sources or reliance on others for your fulfillment, you will perpetually elude the attainment of happiness. Relying on someone will merely nurture your tendency towards codependency. To initiate transformation in your life, it is imperative that you cease the practice of making justifications and assume accountability for every decision and endeavor you undertake.

Indeed, it is important to bear in mind that one is not accountable for every occurrence in one's life. Certain occurrences can be attributed solely to happenstance or spontaneous acts of aggression. Believing oneself to be accountable for all matters can prove to be an excessively burdensome mindset. Therefore, it is imperative to assess the degree of one's accountability in relation to the occurrences taking place within one's own life. Developing self-awareness is the initial stride towards adopting a responsible lifestyle. With that being said, the majority of individuals will realize the necessity of a complete transformation in order to embrace this lifestyle, which undoubtedly presents considerable challenges. It will be a daunting task, but you don't have to do everything all at once. It is necessary to approach this task systematically.

Take Action

Merely acquiring knowledge will prove insufficient. It is imperative that you apply all the knowledge and skills you have acquired. Indeed, it will be necessary to assume certain calculated risks throughout the course of the endeavor, yet the resulting outcome will undoubtedly prove to be highly worthwhile. Establish and articulate your personal boundaries. Engage in an activity that is novel to you. You are likely to experience some initial discomfort, but rest assured, it is perfectly normal.

The presence of shame frequently accompanies low self-esteem, thereby compounding the challenge of embracing risk-taking due to the apprehension of potential judgment from others.

Upon visiting the gym following an extended absence or for the initial occasion, it will become apparent that your muscles experience sensations of tenderness. However, should you desire to persist in attending the gym, it will be necessary to confront and endure such muscular discomfort; yet, in due course, it shall subside. The same applies to your self-esteem. Once one embarks upon a course of action, the inevitable consequence is the emergence of self-doubt or anxiety. However, it is imperative that you persist in your current endeavors, thereby alleviating the sensation of constraint that has been pervading your journey. You will experience significantly reduced resentments as a result of engaging in proactive measures, leading to a simplification of your interpersonal dynamics.

Therefore, I suggest commencing the process of compiling a roster of tasks that have accumulated over a significant duration, and proceed to undertake them in a sequential manner. Do not defer to others, as it is solely your responsibility to confront your apprehensions, for it is your own existence that is at stake.

WHAT IS NARCISSISTIC SUPPLY

The establishment of a secure attachment during early childhood sets a firm basis for the entirety of an individual's lifespan. It engenders a sense of "assurance and reliance on the inherent integrity of myself, yourself, and our collective." This establishment of a secure attachment is facilitated through the fusion of introspection, alignment, compassionate understanding, and affection between the maternal figure (or another principal caretaker) and the infant. It arises from the mother's presence, unwavering consistency, kindness, reassurance, and soothing behavior. Through the development of a secure attachment, an individual acquires the ability to place trust in others and cultivate enduring affection throughout the course of their lifetime.

Individuals with narcissistic traits lack an understanding of how to place trust in the inherent goodwill present within themselves, others, and the collective. Instead, narcissistic individuals prioritize self-preservation above considerations for others. Due to the narcissist's lack of capacity for establishing healthy interpersonal connections, he resorts to employing a relational framework that serves his own self-preservation needs. Instead of seeking genuine emotional bonds, a narcissist actively pursues what is known as "narcissistic supply."

Individuals exhibiting narcissistic tendencies often experience a specific type of trauma during their early years, commonly associated with interpersonal abuse. During a critical period in their early childhood, these individuals did not establish a healthy emotional bond or did not receive the adequate level of affection and care they needed. As a result, he acquired the ability to navigate relationships through a quasi-barter system, as he had not fully internalized the conventional skills essential for genuine human connection.

Narcissistic supply refers to the provision of gratification or validation by others, which is exchanged for the opportunity to maintain a relationship with a narcissist. Essentially, when a young child lacks adequate attunement, emotional soothing, and protection, they develop self-protective skills as a means of survival. These techniques for coping and adapting to challenging situations manifest as the manipulation of emotions and the cultivation of alter egos.

Acknowledge that individuals who have experienced early attachment trauma exhibit a certain degree of developmental delay, especially in the realm of interpersonal connections.

Have you ever observed how your significant other exhibits behaviors reminiscent of a toddler throwing a tantrum? This might be due to his emotional response being activated by a perceived lack of satisfaction with his desires, leading him to revert to an earlier stage of psychological growth that he has not fully progressed through.

In summary, it can be stated that individuals with narcissistic tendencies have not undergone comprehensive progression in the different phases of early childhood development, thereby leading to a hindered advancement of their emotional maturity.

Narcissists are never satisfied. After obtaining the narcissistic supply momentarily, they quickly experience a void once more, as the gratification is not enduring. The emotional reservoir of a narcissist is perpetually depleted or lacking, akin to a situation where the supply of narcissistic nourishment is akin to a tank that has punctures at its base. Despite your utmost efforts to express affection towards your narcissistic counterpart, your endeavors shall forever fall short of their insatiable desire for adoration.

What are several prevalent manifestations of narcissistic supply?

Attention

Compliments/Praise

Accomplishments, such as winning

Experiencing a sense of authority (exerting influence over you)

Experiencing a sense of autonomy (having the ability to exert control over oneself and, subsequently, the surrounding environment)

A compulsive substance or activity.

Sex

Affective energy (can be positive or negative)

The list is not comprehensive, and the phenomenon of narcissistic supply can manifest in distinct ways based on the individuals involved.

What are some things the supplier of this narcissistic "food" can do to feed the narcissist?

Do whatever he wants

Lose your autonomy; yourself

Praise him /compliment him

Be a good "object"

Be compliant

Be controllable

Give up your power

In what manner do narcissists acquire this supply from their "victims"? They employ key tactics, namely seduction, manipulation, gaslighting, outbursts of anger, and bullying conduct.

"Comprehend this undeniable reality:

In a narcissistic encounter, it can be observed that psychologically, there exists solely one individual. The co-narcissist is effectively effaced in this situation, with the narcissistic individual's experience being the sole focus of significance (Rappaport, 2005).

The application of this quote to the concept of narcissistic supply becomes apparent upon observation. The sole purpose underlying this relationship is that each individual involved aims to cater to the needs of the narcissist. This mode of psychological manipulation proves effective, as it induces a temporary, albeit fleeting, sense of security for all parties involved, thereby rendering them susceptible to the narcissist's influence.

Narcissistic supply refers to any alternative source that temporarily provides a sense of gratification.

It is highly probable that this "food" is presented in its authentic state.

The neurotransmitter dopamine, which is commonly known as the "pleasure-inducing" brain chemical.

The narcissist's true longing and continual necessity lies in genuine human connection. However, considering the absence of said supply poses a significant danger to the narcissist's psychological well-being, he has developed the ability to acknowledge and rely upon narcissistic supply as his main source of nourishment.

Chapter 6: Strategies for Protection against Gaslighting

Drawing conclusions about a country or its people based solely on the contents of a single book one has read would not be considered prudent or wise. That is precisely the modus operandi of individuals who engage in gaslighting. They accentuate an imperfection (which may or may not be accurate regarding your character) and endeavor to persuade you to embrace it.

The gaslighter selectively fixates on a solitary narrative from the entirety of one's life, incessantly reiterating it until one eventually internalizes it as truth. By deliberately selecting a particular narrative, often a negative one, and perpetually replaying it, your concentration and attentiveness become fixated on that unfavorable element. You will come across circumstances in which the gaslighter's malevolent narrative appears to be accurate, thereby causing you to gradually contemplate the legitimacy of such a story.

A gaslighter can engage in gaslighting without necessitating an intimate or proximity-based relationship with the individual they are targeting. For instance, they may occupy positions such as your supervisor, subordinate, or coworker. As these individuals possess the ability to assess your performance directly, their influence has the potential to engender a significant level of uncertainty concerning your capabilities. Typically, gaslighters do not overtly dismantle your perceptions; rather, they tend to engage in the systematic analysis and deconstruction of your perspectives and convictions. Therefore, although someone may refrain from directly disparaging you, they can still achieve a comparable outcome by adopting a "realistic" perspective on your capabilities and limitations. They shall persist in retelling the narrative of your insufficiency until you internalize it.

Engaging in denial is the most detrimental course of action one can take when harboring suspicions of being subjected to gaslighting. It is imperative that you attune yourself to your instincts and place absolute faith in them, as the gaslighter consistently endeavors to undermine this essential aspect of your being. This chapter presents valuable suggestions that can be employed to safeguard oneself against succumbing to the deceptive tactics perpetrated by gaslighters.

Strategies for Safeguarding Against Gaslighting in the Workplace

If you harbor suspicions regarding someone engaging in gaslighting behavior within your workplace, it is advisable to first ascertain this fact prior to initiating any course of action. It is advisable to exercise caution before acting hastily to prevent inadvertent verification of any unfounded notions.

Here is a method to definitively ascertain whether an individual is attempting to manipulate you through gaslighting within a professional setting. If one consistently finds oneself burdened with excessive workload either in an attempt to demonstrate competence or due to being assigned tasks that fall beyond the scope of one's designated responsibilities (which may at times be demeaning), it is possible that one is encountering the phenomenon of gaslighting in the workplace. If an individual intentionally undermines your work, manipulates deadlines to cause you to miss them, or creates confusion about your responsibilities, they are exhibiting prominent indications of engaging in gaslighting behavior.

Another discreet indication to be alert for is declining opportunities, not due to personal disinterest or feelings of inadequacy, but rather in an attempt to evade potential criticism or belittlement. The colleague whom you suspect may confront you with opposition should you accept these opportunities is likely engaging in manipulative tactics known as gaslighting. It is possible that they exhibited signs of displeasure regarding your professional advancement, engaged in covert criticism while passing by your workspace, mocked you in the presence of other colleagues, and attempted to undermine your reputation in the eyes of your superiors. In order to mitigate the occurrence of subsequent emotional attacks, you gradually retreat into your personal reserve and succumb to the influence they exert over your conduct in the workplace.

Here are some additional factors to remain vigilant for:

● Withholding your inclusion (from significant meetings or social gatherings with colleagues).

- Consistently interweaving each conversation with references to previous mistakes you have made. - Perpetually connecting any conversation

to prior instances where you have erred.
- Unfailingly tying every other discussion to occasions where you have acted erroneously in the past.

Engaging in the act of making disparaging comments towards you upon voicing a complaint. As an illustration, it is evident that you struggle with adhering to instructions.

• Engaging in gossip and disseminating unfounded rumors concerning your character.

• Disputing the veracity of their statement. • Challenging the accuracy of their claims. • Contesting the validity of their assertion. • Contradicting the information they provided. • Refuting what they have stated.

If you observe a regular and recurring pattern of disruptive conduct from an individual in a position of authority over you, a colleague, a supervisor, or any other person within your professional sphere, it is reasonable to deduce that they are engaging in the practice of gaslighting towards you.

I would suggest that your subsequent course of action is to maintain a comprehensive record of your formal engagements. Record and archive all instructions and communications, ensuring that you possess duplicate copies of both written and digital correspondences. In the case of oral communication, it is advisable to secure the presence of a witness or request that the information be documented in writing, whenever feasible. As an illustration, suppose that your boss, who engages in gaslighting behavior, is feeling favorable and expresses that you may have a day off upon finishing your current task. It would be a prudent course of action to seize this opportunity to request written documentation of their agreement while they are still in a positive disposition. Gaslighters will encounter significant challenges in deceiving you if you possess such indisputable evidence. In the event that they refuse to acknowledge or attempt to deceive you in order to cause confusion, rely on your sources of evidence to establish the truth and preserve your mental composure and self-assurance.

In the event that the individual engaging in gaslighting continues to persist in their conduct, you have the option to escalate the matter and bring it to the attention of the Human Resources department or upper-level management personnel. However, it is imperative that you possess indisputable evidence (whether in the form of physical or digital documentation) prior to lodging a formal complaint. It is also imperative to adhere to established protocols with regard to filing grievances within your organization. It is essential to ensure compliance with all applicable regulations while prioritizing one's personal safety.

Engaging in discussions with select colleagues in the workplace with the intention of ascertain whether they are encountering similar circumstances can prove beneficial; however, such course of action may not always yield favorable outcomes. It is possible that an individual with whom you engage in conversation may act as an informant, thereby exacerbating the situation. You may be subject to allegations of engaging in gossip and defamation, and such accusations would not be unfounded. Should you feel compelled to discuss the matter with your fellow colleagues, exercise caution and ensure the trustworthiness and discretion of those with whom you choose to confide.

An additional efficacious measure that can be taken to safeguard oneself against subsequent assaults from a gaslighter is the application of straightforwardness when engaging with them. Notify them of your comprehension regarding their objectives, while expressing your reluctance to engage in their manipulative tactics. Frequently, individuals who engage in gaslighting employ significant efforts to conceal their manipulative behaviors. Therefore, by effectively revealing their obfuscation, one may succeed in deterring their unwanted presence. For instance, instead of partaking in fruitless debates through the employment of defensive expressions like "I did not" or "I am not," rephrase your statements in a manner that promotes assertiveness. One could convey a similar message using a more formal tone by stating, "I decline to engage in a debate with you." Please clarify your desires and outline the collaborative steps we can undertake to achieve them."

Gaslighting extends beyond exclusively intimate relationships. It occurs with alarming regularity within the professional environment, often surpassing the extent to which we are willing to acknowledge. However, refrain from accepting it solely with the intention of avoiding conflicts. Hold your ground and refuse to let others convince you that you are easily influenced.

Diagnosis Of Narcissism

There exists a cognitive assessment instrument known as the Narcissistic Personality Inventory (NPI), which employs a set of forced choice questions to effectively gauge narcissism within diverse populations. Additionally, the diagnostic instrument known as the Millon Clinical Multiaxial Inventory (MCMI) serves as a reliable tool predominantly employed by medical practitioners to diagnose Narcissistic Personality Disorder (NPD) in individual cases. These tools can provide assistance, however, they are insufficient on their own. They should be utilized alongside assessments of patient conduct. To receive a diagnosis of NPD and access appropriate treatment, it is necessary for a patient's condition to align with the specific diagnostic criteria outlined in the Diagnostic and Statistical Manual of Mental Disorders (DSM-5).

NPD Behavioral Characteristics

The expressions of narcissistic personality disorder exhibit a profound level of self-absorption, occasionally described as an erotic fixation, encompassing an intense focus on physical attractiveness. If an individual is diagnosed with narcissistic personality disorder (NPD), it typically stems from the observations made by a psychiatrist or another appropriately qualified healthcare professional, who notices the patient consistently demonstrating an inability to experience affection or empathy towards others, focusing solely on themselves instead. Frequently, they are incapable of affording their significant other, friends, and other family members the love, companionship, and concern necessary for fostering a healthy reciprocal relationship.

Additionally, the individual demonstrates a complete absence of empathy, displaying a disregard for the emotions of others and a willful ignorance of the concerns and values held by those around them. They have consistently lacked the ability to truly understand or express empathy towards others, particularly those facing challenging circumstances. Indeed, the narcissist harbors solely their own outlook when it comes to perceiving the world.

In the context of Narcissistic Personality Disorder (NPD), individuals afflicted with this condition frequently exhibit an exaggerated sense of self-assurance and self-importance, which is often disconnected from objective reality. They will perceive their appearance and abilities as significantly superior to their actual state, yet they possess an inability to handle even the most minor form of criticism. They will yearn for and even insist on receiving accolades and adulation from individuals within their personal sphere.

The narcissist exploits the efforts of others to fulfill their needs.

In reference to the aforementioned earlier paper authored by Martin Buber, it was observed by Buber that individuals with narcissistic traits perceive others as mere instruments to be exploited in the pursuit of their own objectives, rather than regarding them as fellow human beings of equal stature. They will exploit others as means to their own objectives, with no regard for the potential consequences inflicted upon the individuals involved.

Insufficient Establishment of Suitable Limits

This particular mindset of regarding individuals as mere tools can lead to a peculiar situation wherein the narcissist is unable to differentiate between their own identity and that of others. Hence, the narcissist perceives others as a mere extension of their own being and holds the belief that the sole purpose of others' existence is to fulfill their own needs. In the event that it is revealed that the individuals in question serve no such purpose, the narcissist fails to acknowledge their presence.

Indeed, it is true. The narcissist does not acknowledge the existence of others unless they are solely dedicated to fulfilling the narcissist's every requirement. This condition is commonly referred to as boundary recognition deficiency. Put simply, individuals with narcissistic tendencies view others as mere extensions of themselves and anticipate that these individuals will conform to their expectations and meet every single one of their demands. There exists no demarcation between the narcissist and individuals surrounding them. For individuals whom narcissists perceive as genuine extensions of their own being, they excessively bestow flattery and admiration without justification, thereby striving to uphold the validation of their exaggerated sense of self-importance.

Oblivious

An additional characteristic exhibited by the narcissist is a dearth of consciousness and introspection. They are under the complete absence of knowledge regarding their mental illness, demonstrating a profound lack of awareness towards the consequences their behavior imposes on those around them. This can pose significant challenges in the treatment of individuals with narcissistic tendencies. Additionally, this circumstance renders it exceedingly challenging for them to engage in conventional interpersonal connections with individuals. Their entire social engagement revolves around self-centeredness, rendering the establishment of any mutually beneficial relationship highly challenging for others involved.

Deficit in Apt Emotional Expression

The narcissist lacks the capacity to experience appropriate emotions in their relationships as their focus is solely centered on themselves, devoid of concern for others. In addition to the absence of conventional affectionate sentiments, their emotional response to regret, when warranted, is either completely suppressed or perpetually elusive. When inflicting emotional harm upon others, and even resorting to violent acts, individuals should experience a sense of shame and remorse, yet an absence of such emotions is apparent. They lead a life wherein they refrain from issuing apologies, seeking forgiveness, or displaying remorse for causing emotional or physical harm to others.

On the contrary, in instances where an individual performs an exceptional act on behalf of the narcissist, typically prompting feelings of gratitude and an appropriate expression of thanks, the narcissist will refrain from displaying any signs of appreciation. This phenomenon occurs due to the narcissist's expectation that all individuals in their life would invariably perform exceptional actions for the narcissist, rendering any deviation from this norm as unconventional. Indeed, as we shall delve into subsequently, the predominant sentiment experienced in the absence of catering to and idolizing the narcissist is known as injury and rage.

www.ingramcontent.com/pod-product-compliance
Lightning Source LLC
Chambersburg PA
CBHW050241120526
44590CB00016B/2177